MY FAVORITE
PROGRAM
ALBUM

33 Selected Piano Solos

Revised and Edited by
MAXWELL ECKSTEIN

CARL FISCHER®
65 Bleecker Street, New York, NY 10012

O3198

ISBN 0-8258-0161-3

CONTENTS

Page

ALBENIZ, I.
Tango 33

BACH, J. S.
First Prelude and Fugue from *The Well-
tempered Clavier*, Book I 46

BEETHOVEN, L. van
Adagio from *Sonata* in C sharp Minor,
"Moonlight" 12

CHOPIN, F.
Nocturne (E flat Major) 90
Polonaise Militaire 85
Prelude (C Minor) 3
Minute Waltz 36
Waltz in C sharp Minor 40

DEBUSSY, C.
Rêverie 155

GRANADOS, E.
Playera 94

GRIEG, E.
Butterfly, The 114

LISZT, F.
Dreams of Love (*Liebestraume*) 72

MENDELSSOHN, F.
Praeludium 117
Scherzo (E Minor) 56
Spinning Song from *Song without Words* . . 28

MONTI, V.
Czardas 50

MOUSSORGSKY, M.
Hopak 62

Page

MOZART; W. A.
Allegro from *Sonata* in C Major
(K. 545) 16
Fantasia (D Minor) 22
Rondo alla Turca from Sonata in A Major
(K. 331) 4

PADEREWSKI, I. J.
Menuet 133

PALMGREN, S.
May-Night 138

PROKOFIEFF, S.
Peter and the Wolf (Triumphal March) 78

RACHMANINOFF, S.
Polichinelle 141
Prelude (C sharp Minor) 127

RIMSKY-KORSAKOFF, N.
Flight of the Bumblebee from *Tsar Saltan* 122

RUBINSTEIN, A.
Romance (E flat Major) 111

SCARLATTI, D.
Pastorale from *Sonata* No. 1 8

SCHUMANN, R.
Träumerei from *Scenes from Childhood* . . . 20

SIBELIUS, J.
Romance 150
Valse triste 66

SINDING, C.
Rustle of Spring 98

TCHAIKOVSKY, P.
June (Barcarolle) 106

Cover photograph courtesy of Steinway & Sons.

Prelude
in C Minor

F. CHOPIN, Op. 28, No. 20
(1810-1849)

Copyright 1943 by Carl Fischer, Inc., New York

Rondo alla Turca

Sonata in A Major

W. A. MOZART (K. 331)
(1756-1791)

Allegretto (♩ = 132)

a)

a)

O3198

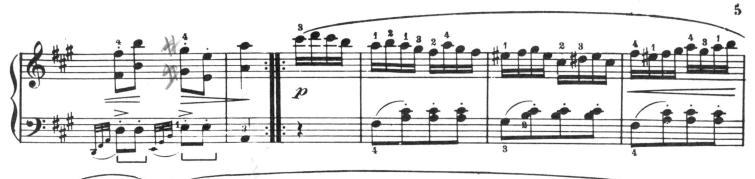

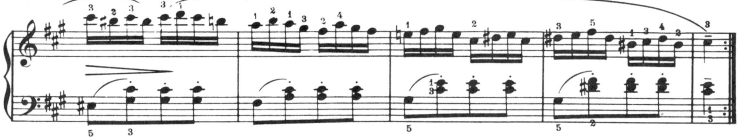

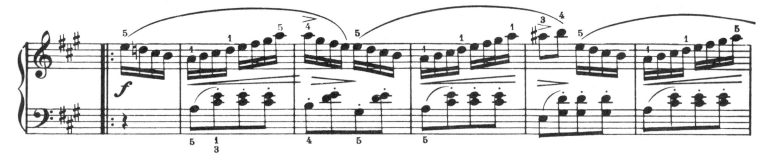

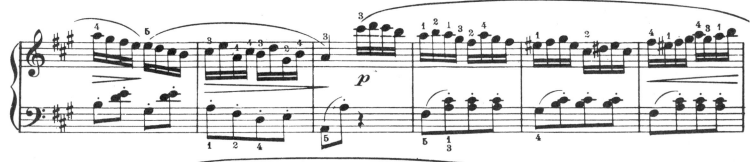

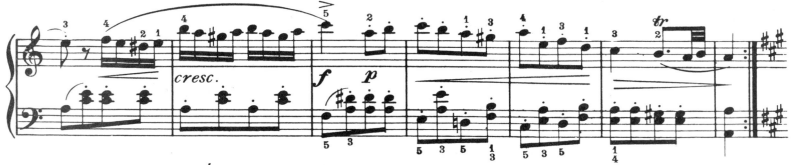

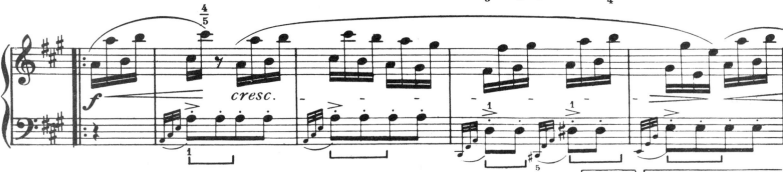

Coda

etc. c) execution here is the
same as shown under b).

O3198

Pastorale
Sonata I

DOMENICO SCARLATTI
(1685-1757)
arr. for Concert use by C. TAUSIG

Allegretto

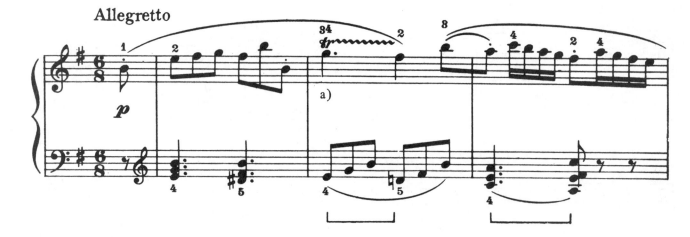

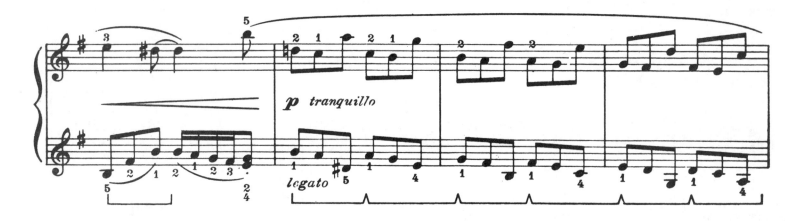

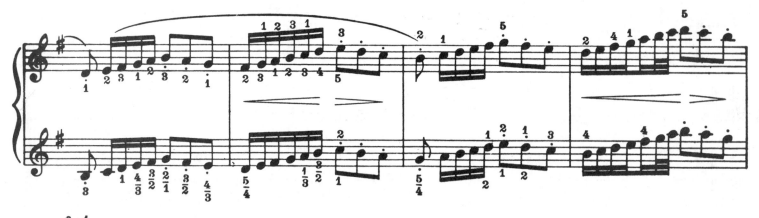

 etc.

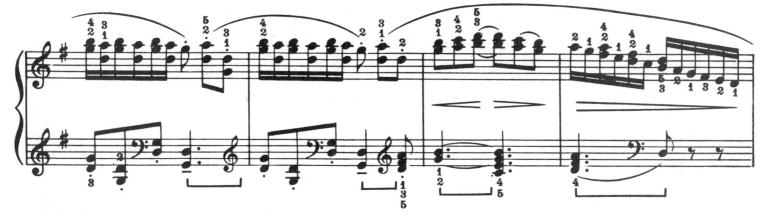

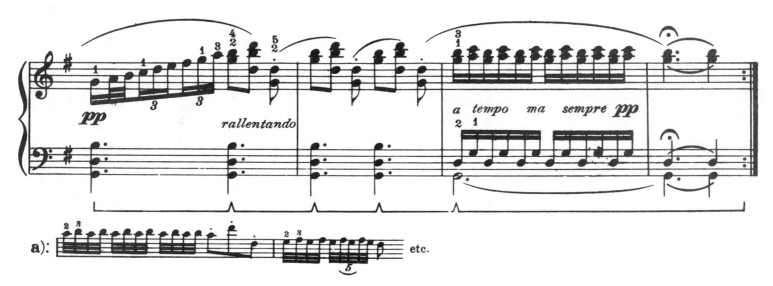

O3198

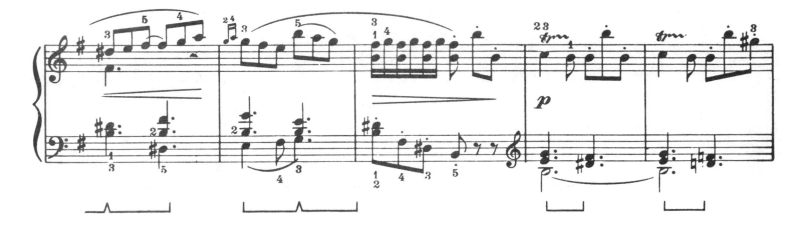

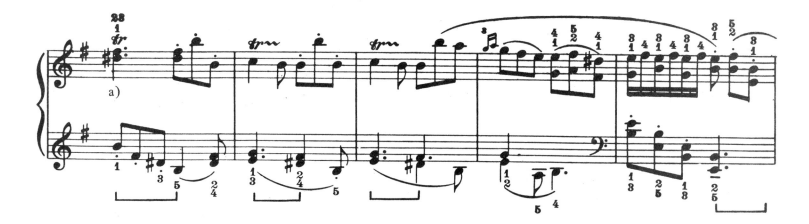

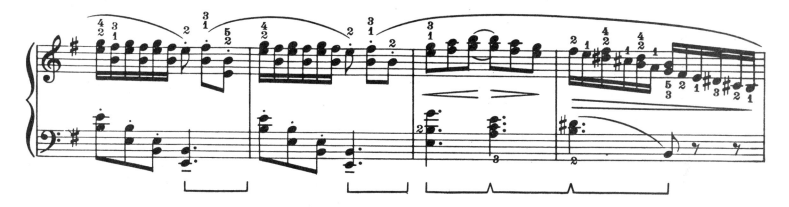

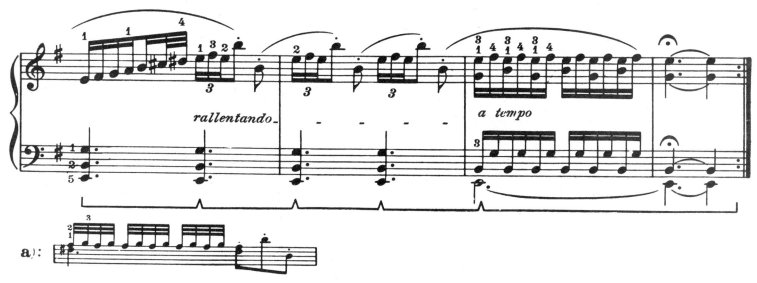

Adagio
Sonata in C sharp Minor
"Moonlight"

LUDWIG VAN BEETHOVEN, Op. 27, No. 2
(1770-1827)

Adagio sostenuto (♩ = 52)

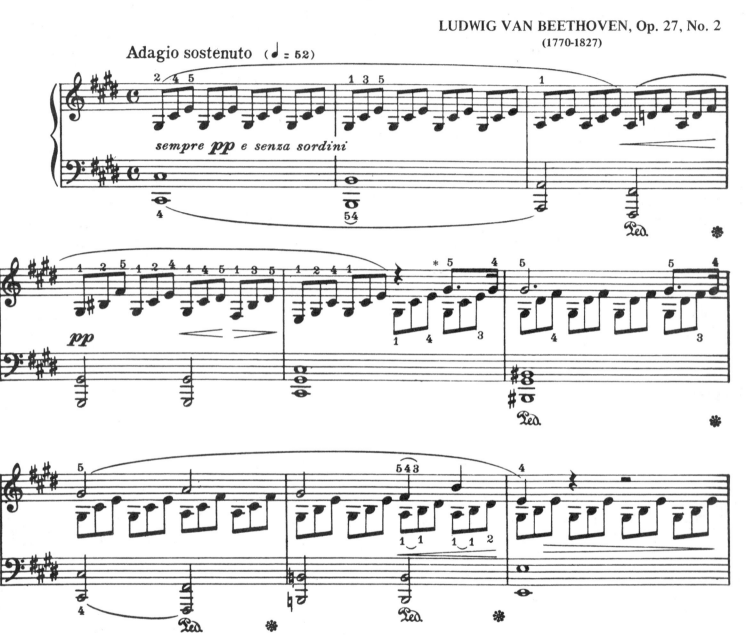

sempre *pp* e senza sordini

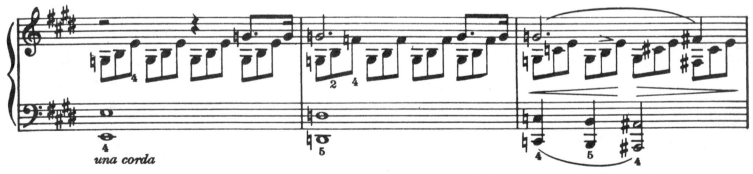

una corda

*) The upper voice to be played somewhat stronger than the accompaniment but with the same soft, veiled-like touch.
Care is to be taken that the accompanying triplets are not played in too uniform a manner.

O3198

Allegro
Sonata in C Major

W. A. MOZART (K. 545)
(1756-1791)

a) *mp* (*mezzo piano*, medium soft) indicates an intermediate degree of tone power between *p* and *mf*.

b)

O3198

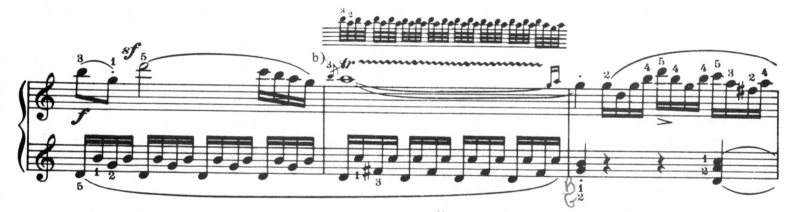

a)

b) easier

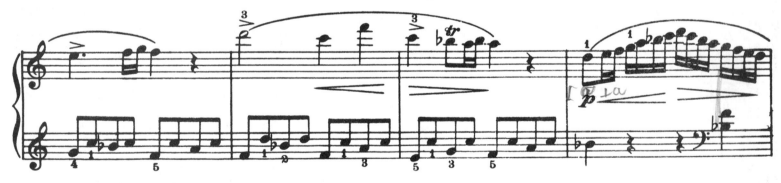

Träumerei
Scenes from Childhood

R. SCHUMANN, Op. 15, No. 7
(1810-1856)

O3198

O3198

Fantasia
in D Minor

W. A. MOZART (K. 397)
(1756-1791)

Copyright 1943 by Carl Fischer, Inc., New York

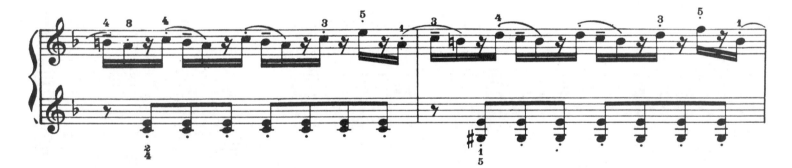

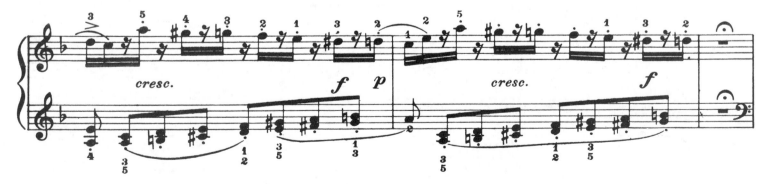

Presto

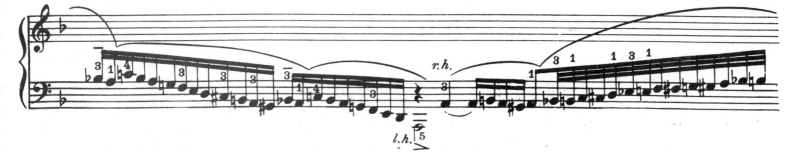

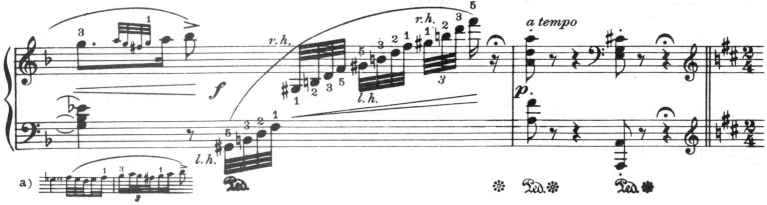

Allegretto (♩ = 108)

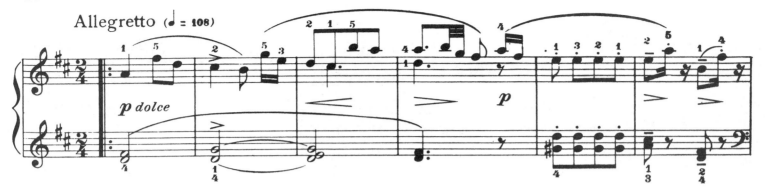

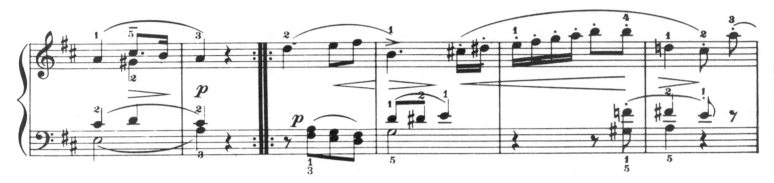

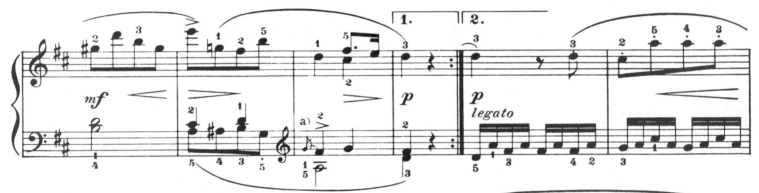

Spinning Song
Song without Words

F. MENDELSSOHN, Op. 67, No. 4
(1809-1847)

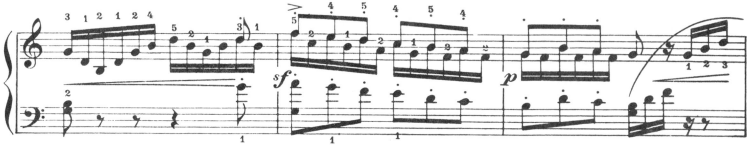

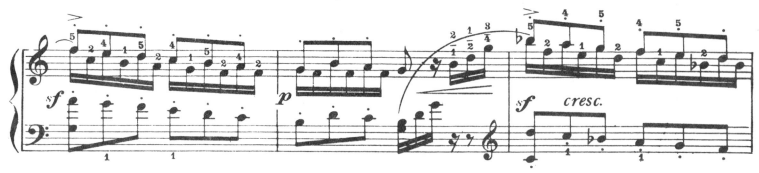

O3198

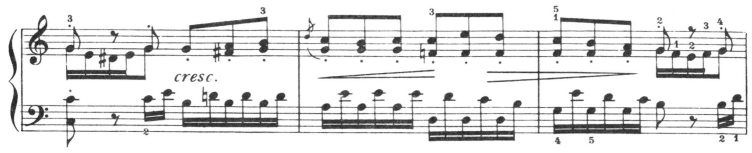

O3198

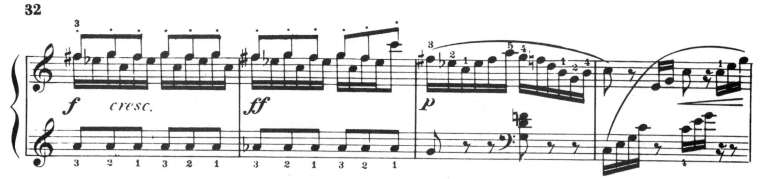

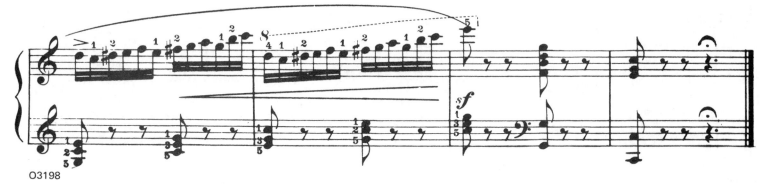

Tango

I. ALBENIZ, Op. 165, No. 2
(1861-1909)

O3198

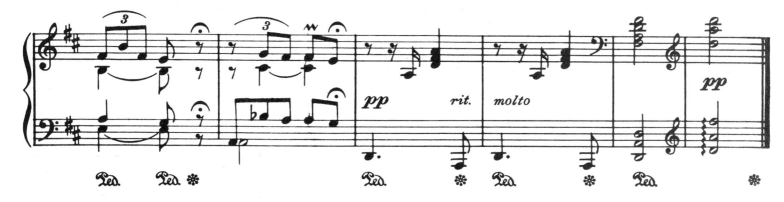

Minute Waltz

F. CHOPIN, Op. 64, No. 1
(1810-1849)

Molto vivace

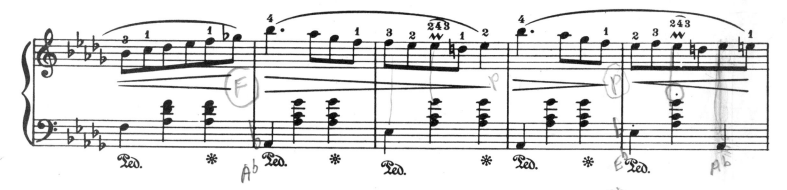

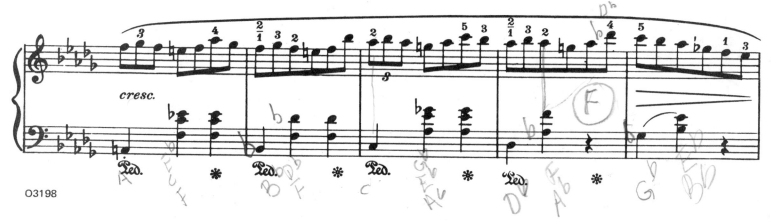

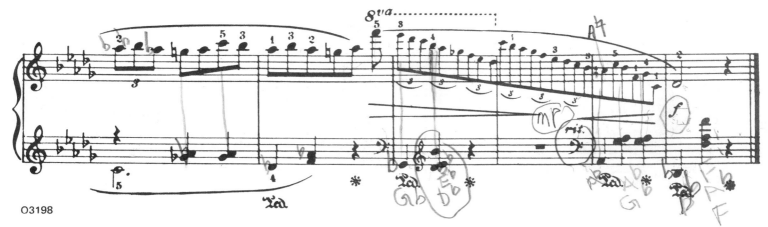

Waltz in C sharp Minor

F. CHOPIN, Op. 64, No. 2
(1810-1849)

Tempo giusto

Più mosso

Più mosso

O3198

Tempo I

Più mosso

First Prelude and Fugue
The Well-tempered Clavier
Prelude I

J. S. BACH (1685-1750)

Moderato

O3198

* Measure 23 may be omitted by the player if he so desires, as this measure cannot be authenticated, and is not found in any of Bach's autographs. It is found only in a manuscript by Schwenke.

Fugue I

O3198

Czardas

V. MONTI
*Arranged for Piano Solo
by GUSTAV SAENGER*

Largo

Largo

Con Pedale

Allegretto vivace

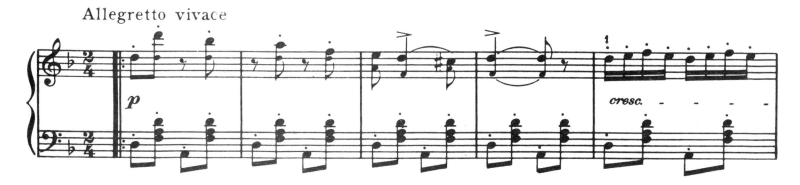

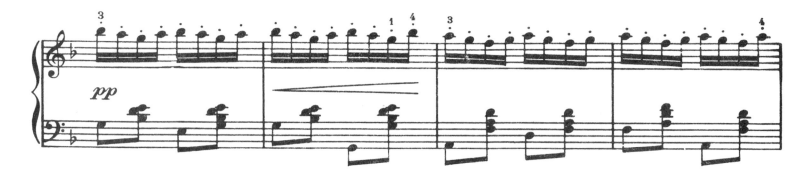

Meno, quasi lento

Allegro vivace

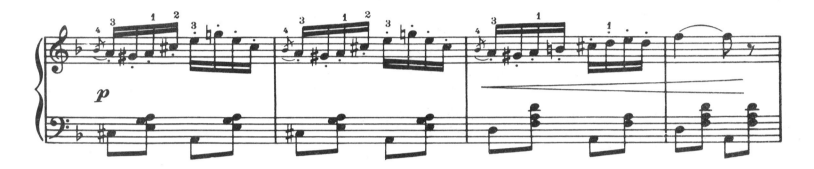

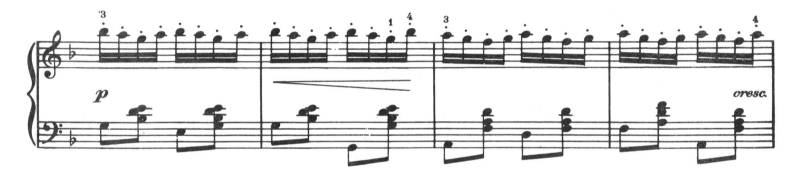

Allegretto

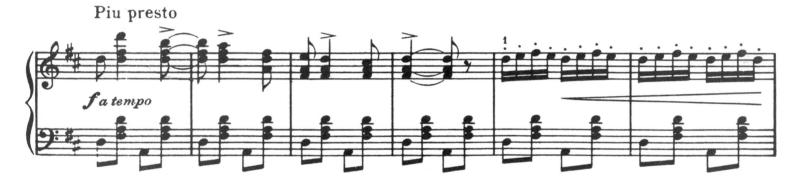

Piu presto

Molto piú vivo

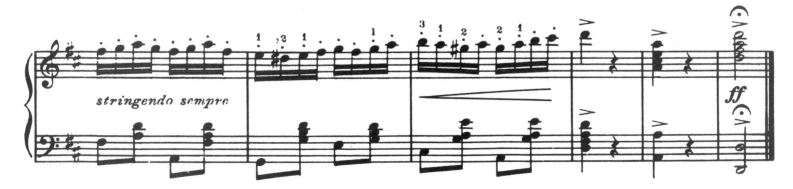

Scherzo

F. MENDELSSOHN, Op. 16, No. 2
(1809-1847)

Copyright 1943 by Carl Fischer, Inc., New York

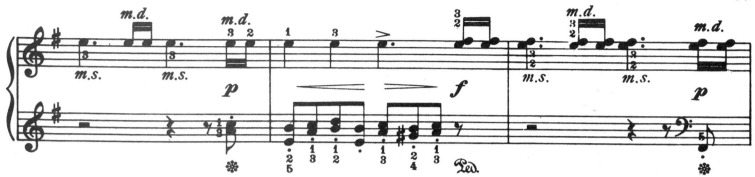

*R. H.
Optional
fingering
O3198

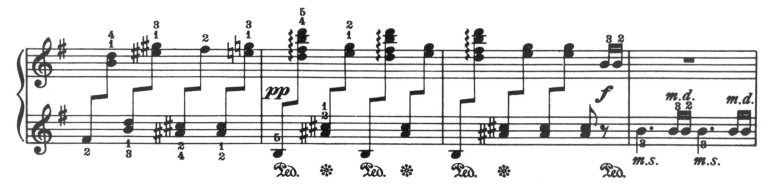

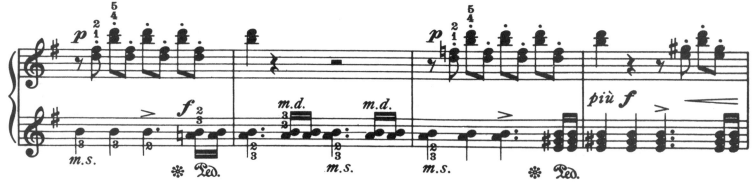

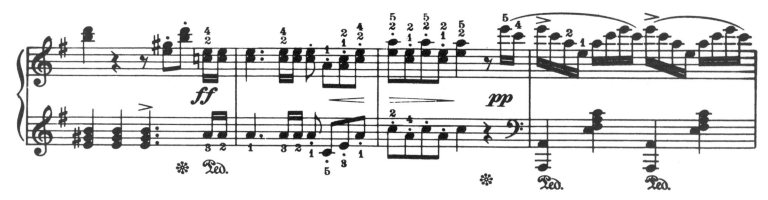

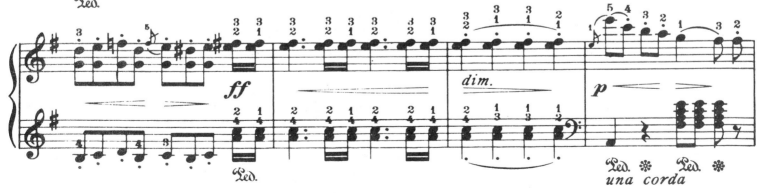

* Similar to ossia on first page.

O3198

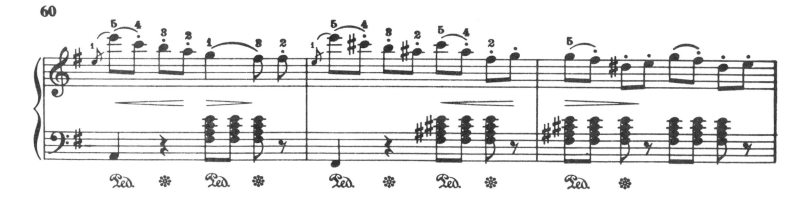

tre corde

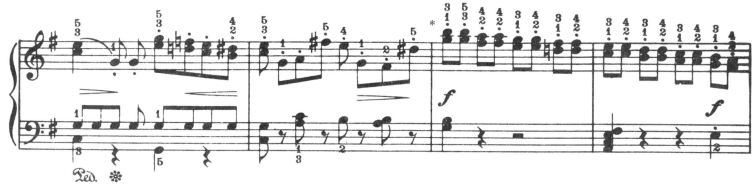

*R.H.
Optional
fingering

una corda

O3198

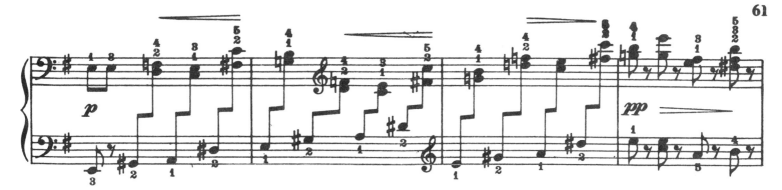

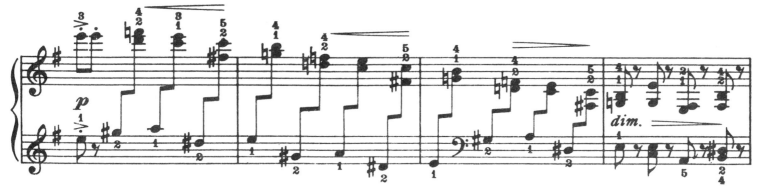

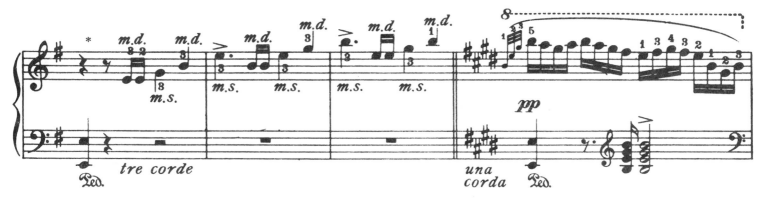

*Ossia

Hopak

MODEST MOUSSORGSKY
(1835-1881)

Allegro vivace

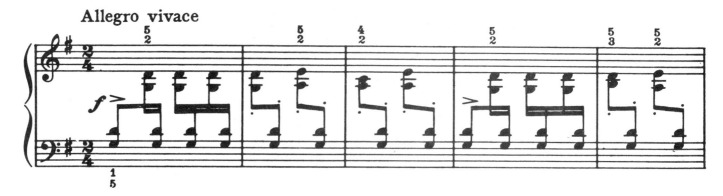

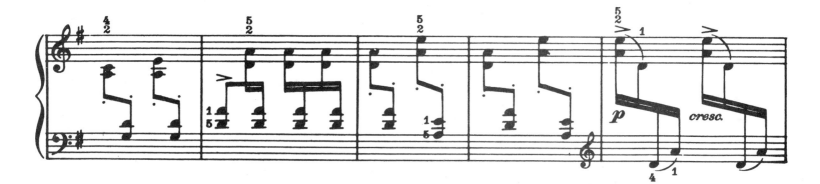

Copyright 1943 by Carl Fischer, Inc., New York

Valse triste
from *Kuolema*

JEAN SIBELIUS, Op. 44
(1865-1957)

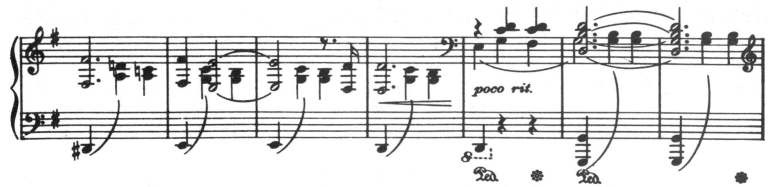

O3198

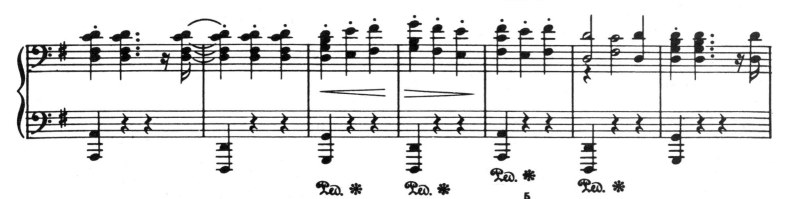

O3198

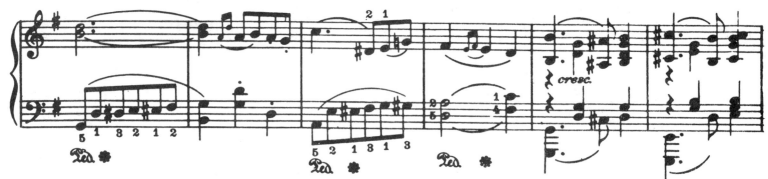

O3198

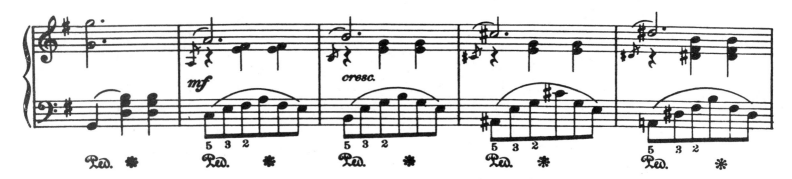

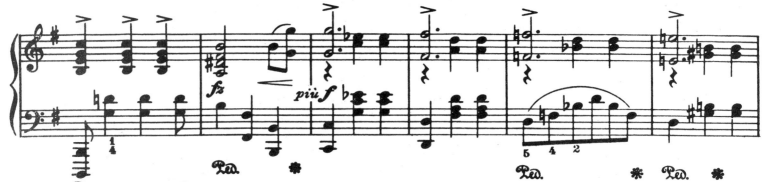

Dreams of Love

Liebesträume
Notturno III

FRANZ LISZT
(1811-1886)

Poco allegro, con affetto

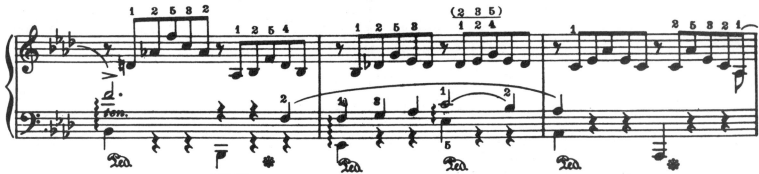

O3198

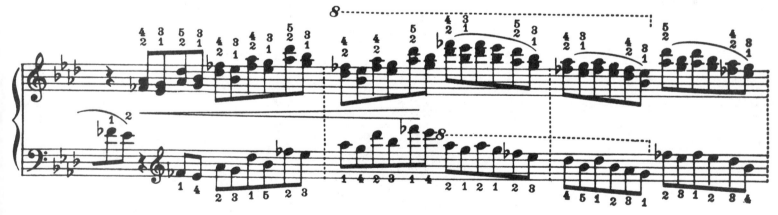

O3198

Più animato e con passione

sempre stringendo

a) Ossia:

etc.

poco a poco — — — — — ritenuto

più smorz. e rit.

Peter and the Wolf
Triumphal March

SERGEI PROKOFIEFF, Op. 67
(1891-1953)

Allegro moderato

O3198

*) Notes in parentheses may be omitted.

O3198

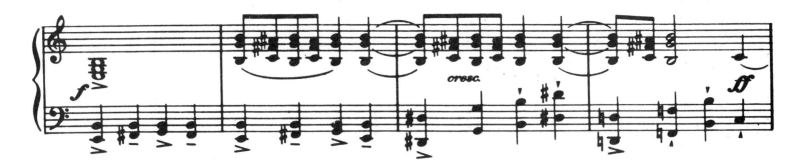

Sostenuto

L'istesso tempo

Poco più mosso

*) Notes in parentheses may be omitted.

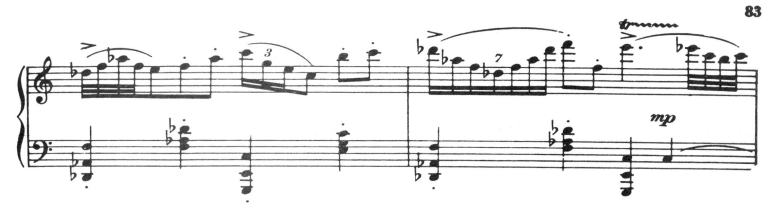

O3198

Andante

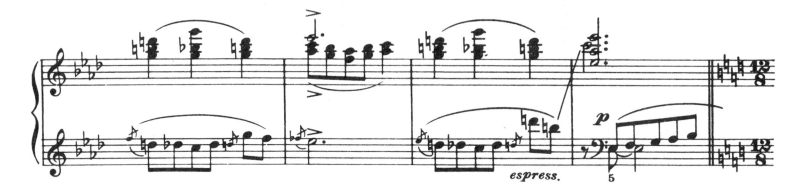

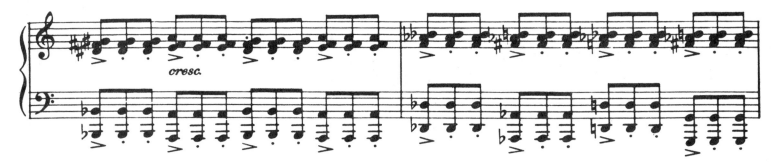

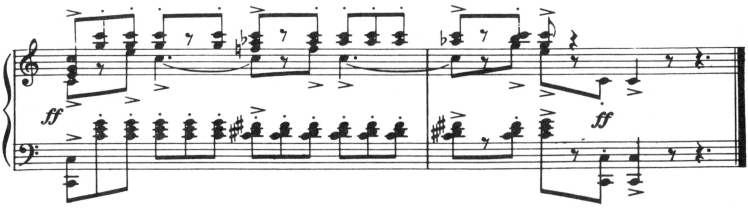

Polonaise Militaire

F. CHOPIN, Op. 40, No. 1
Arranged by Maxwell Eckstein

Allegro con brio

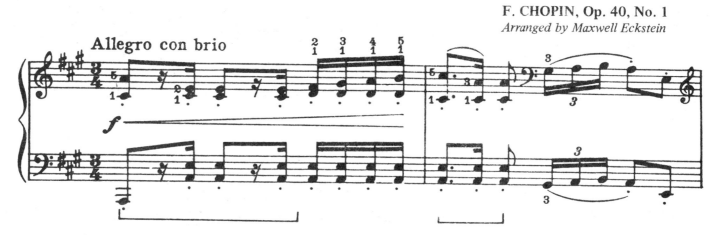

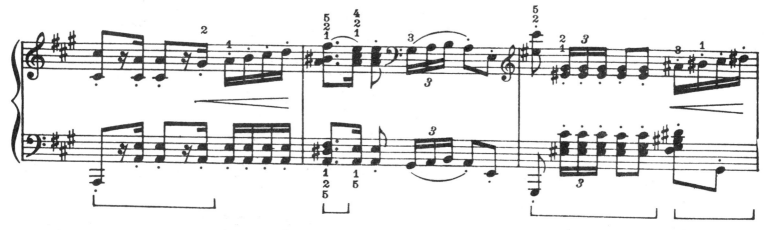

O3198

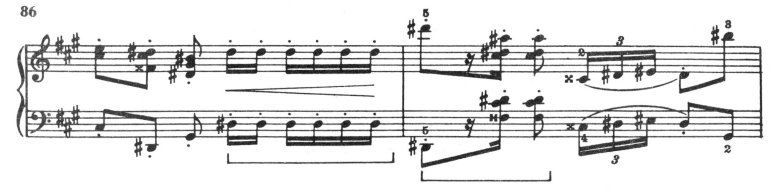

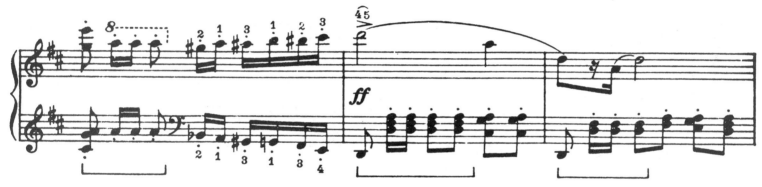

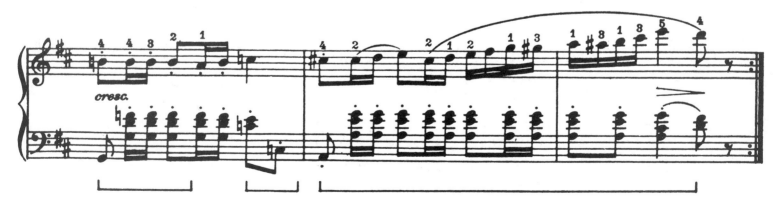

O3198

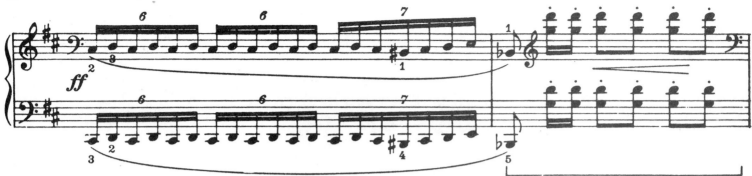

D. C. al Fine

Nocturne
in E flat Major

F. CHOPIN, Op. 9, No. 2
(1810-1849)

Andante (♩.= 44)
espressivo

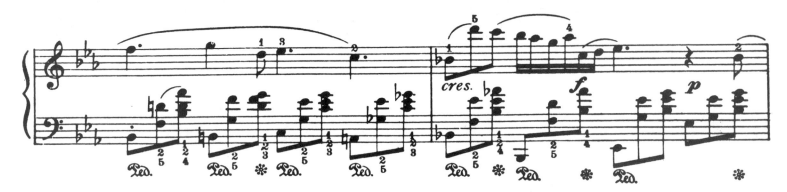

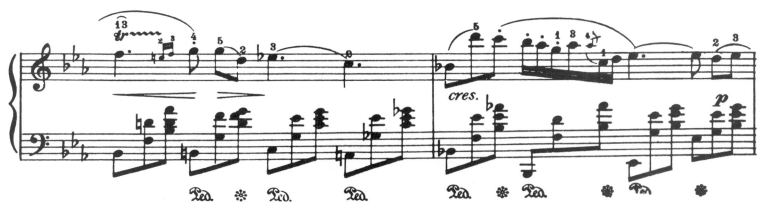

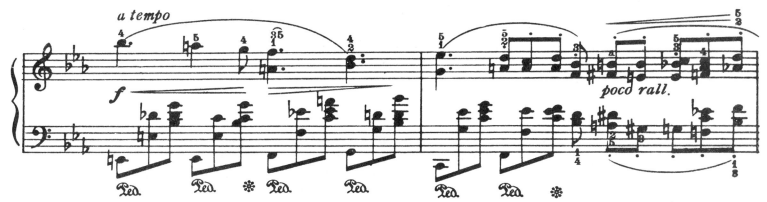

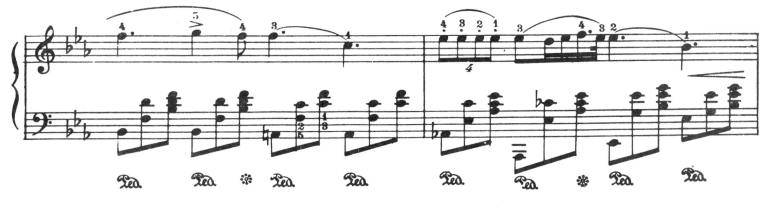

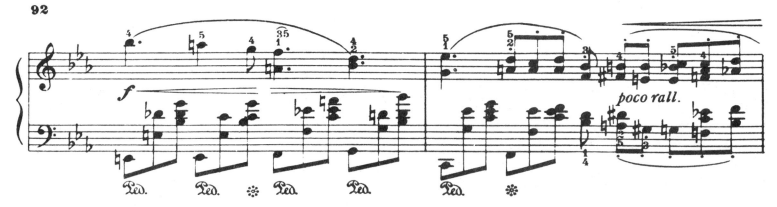

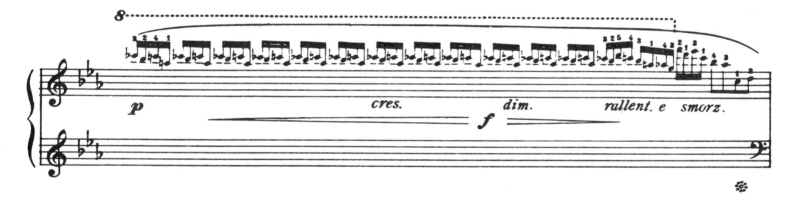

Playera
Spanish Dance

E. GRANADOS, Op. 5, No. 5
(1867-1916)

Andantino, quasi Allegretto

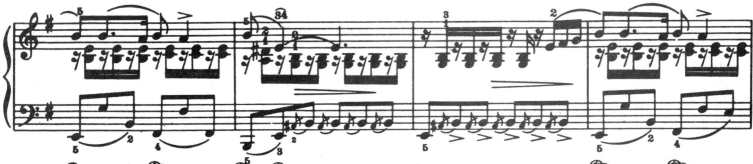

O3198

Rustle of Spring

CHRISTIAN SINDING, Op. 32, No. 3
(1856-1941)

O3198

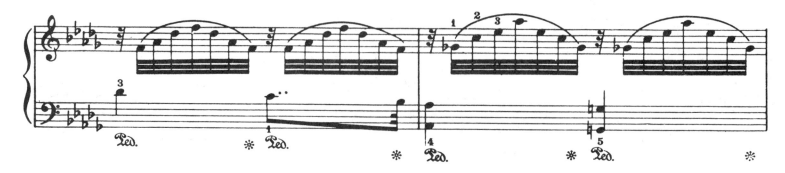

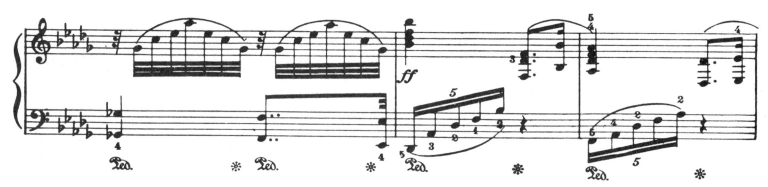

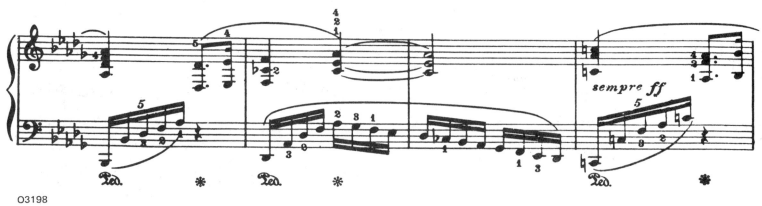

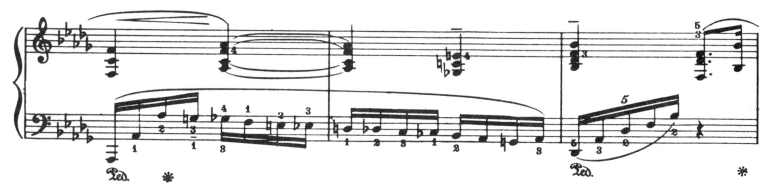

O3198

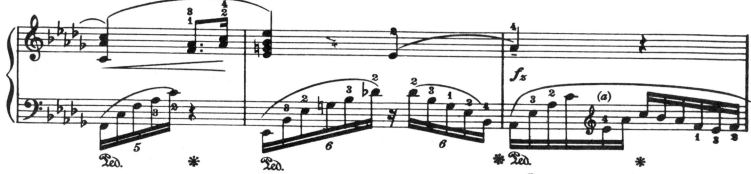

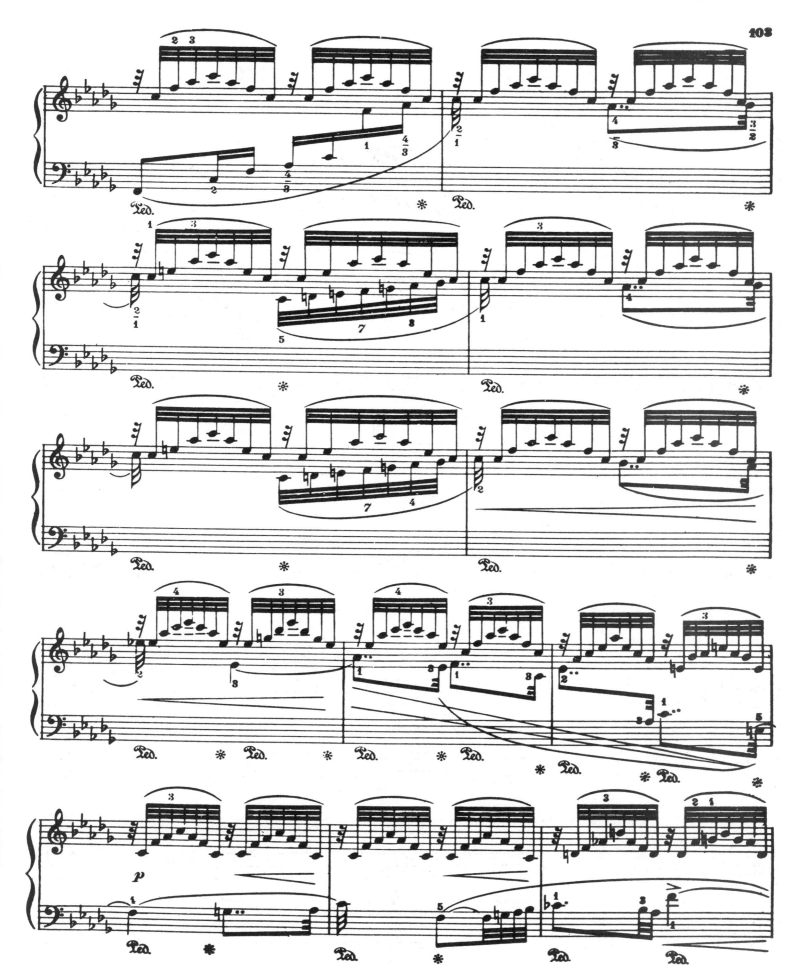

O3198

June
Barcarolle

P. TCHAIKOVSKY, Op. 37, No. 6
(1840-1893)

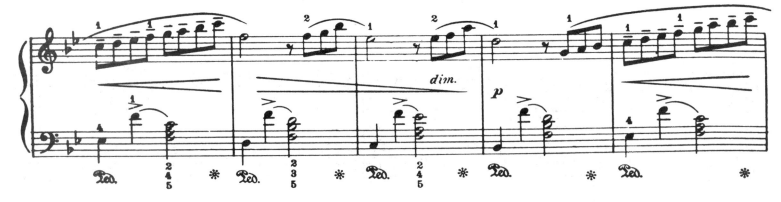

O3198

Romance
in E flat Major

ANTON RUBINSTEIN, Op. 44, No. 1
(1830-1894)

con molto espressione

Moderato

O3198

O3198

O3198

The Butterfly
Le Papillon

E. GRIEG, Op. 43, No. 1
(1843-1907)

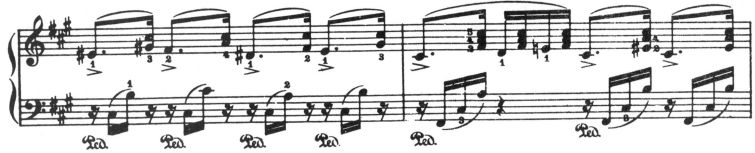

O3198

O3198

Praeludium

F. MENDELSSOHN
(1809-1847)

O3198

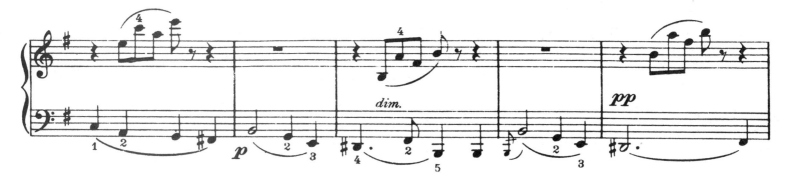

Flight of the Bumblebee

from *Tsar Saltan*

N. RIMSKY-KORSAKOFF (1844-1908)

Arranged by Maxwell Eckstein

O3198

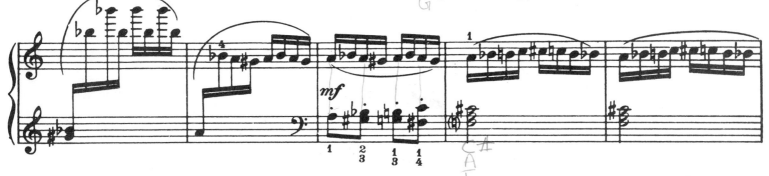

124

O3198

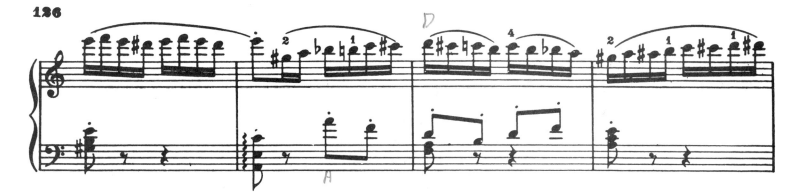

Prelude
in C sharp Minor

SERGEI RACHMANINOFF, Op. 3, No. 2
(1873-1943)

Copyright 1943 by Carl Fischer, Inc., New York

Agitato

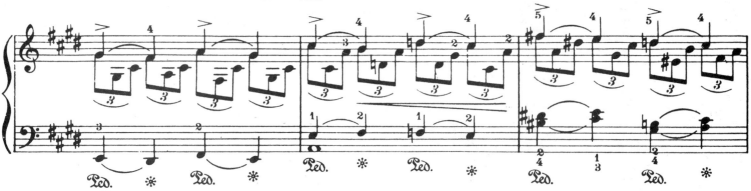

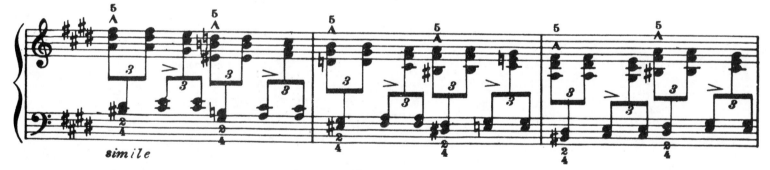

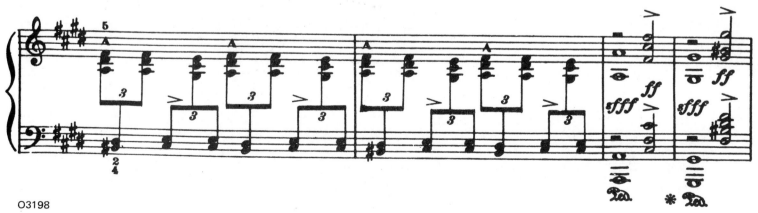

Tempo I°.

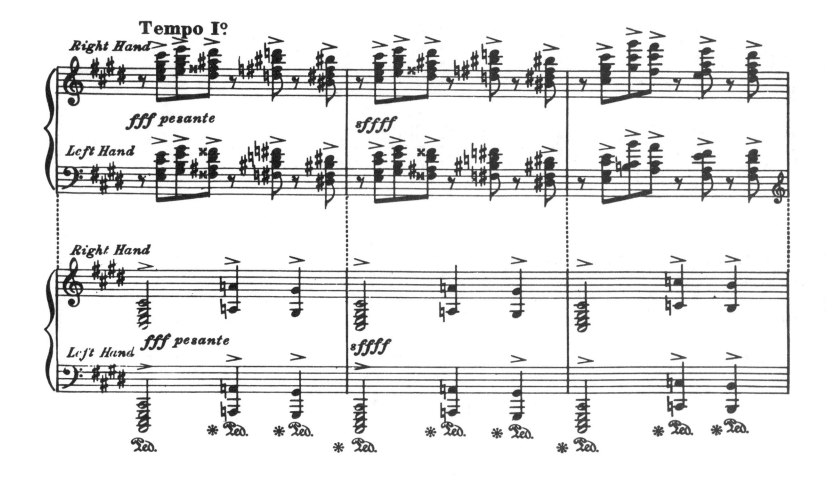

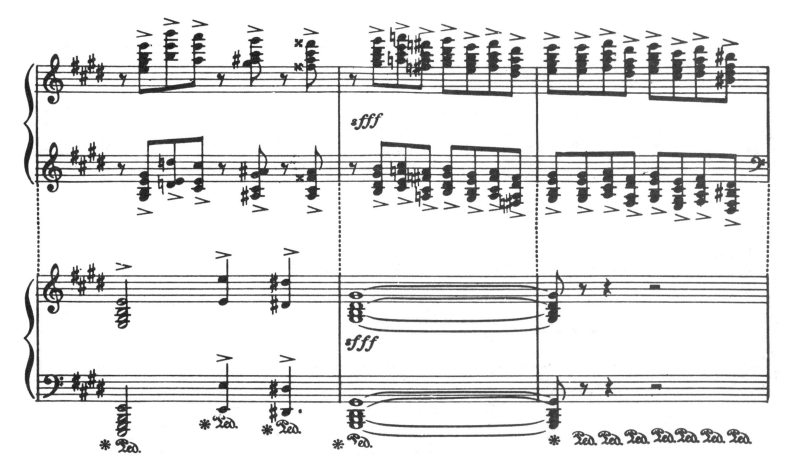

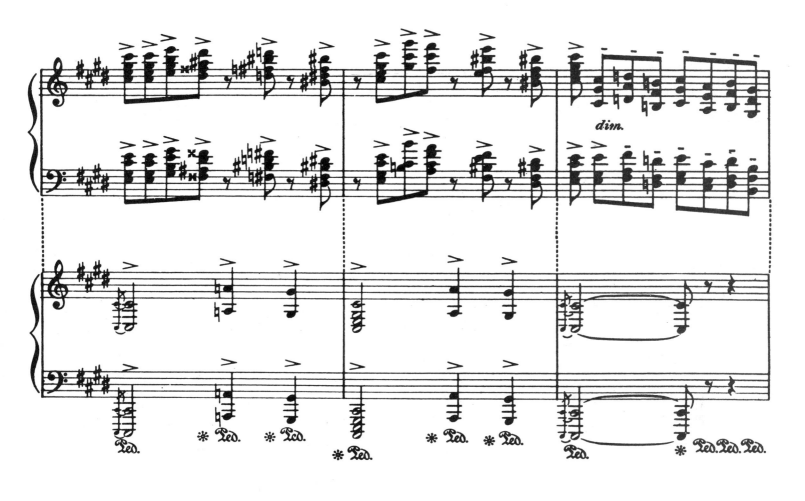

O3198

Menuet - Paderewski, Op. 14

The execution of embellishments as suggested by the editor:

A on p. 133 and on p. 136:

Menuet

I. J. PADEREWSKI, Op. 14
(1859-1941)

Allegretto

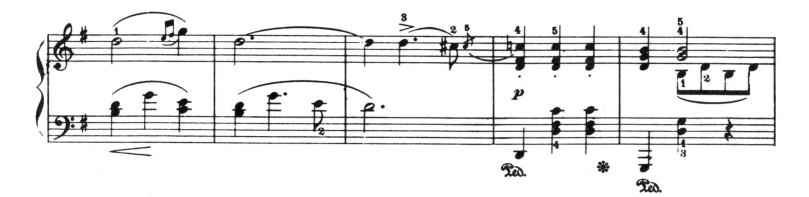

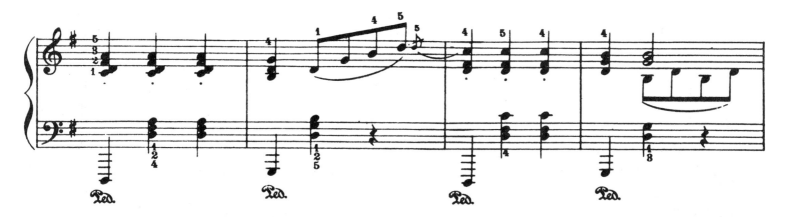

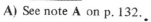

a)

A) See note **A** on p. 132.

O3198

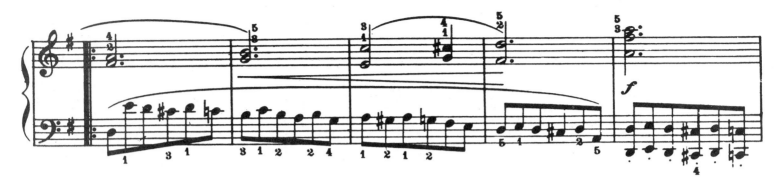

con forza la melodia

B) See note b) on p. 132.

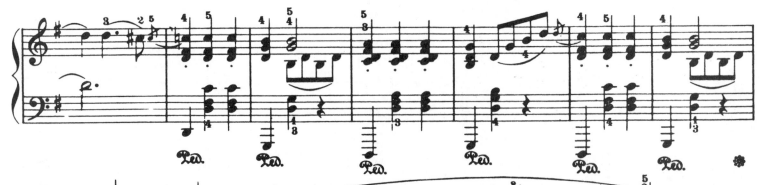

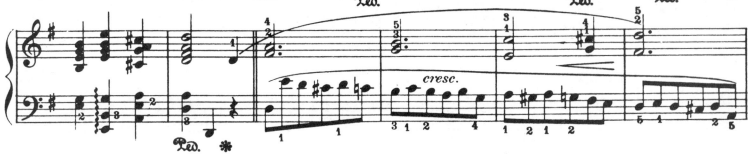

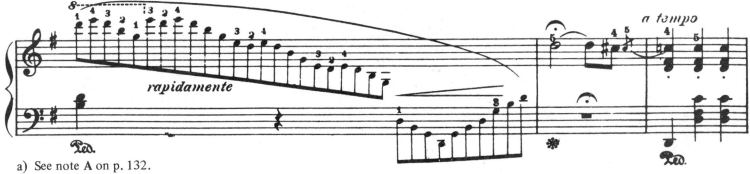

a) See note A on p. 132.

CODA
Vivo

C) See note c) on p. 132.

May-Night

SELIM PALMGREN; Op. 27, No. 4
(1878-1951)

Lento e Placido

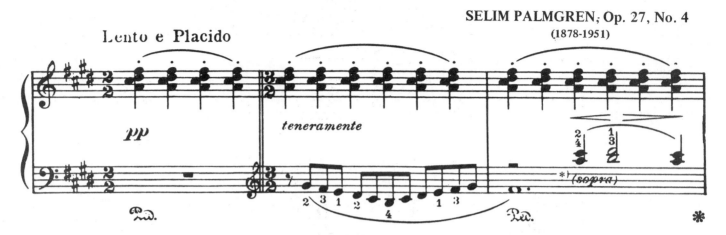

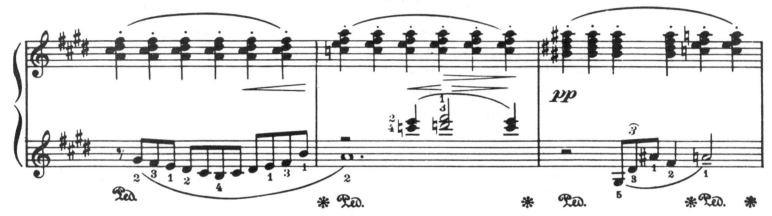

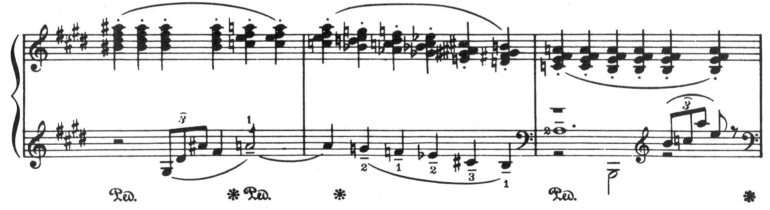

*) Meaning to lift the left hand above the right.

O3198

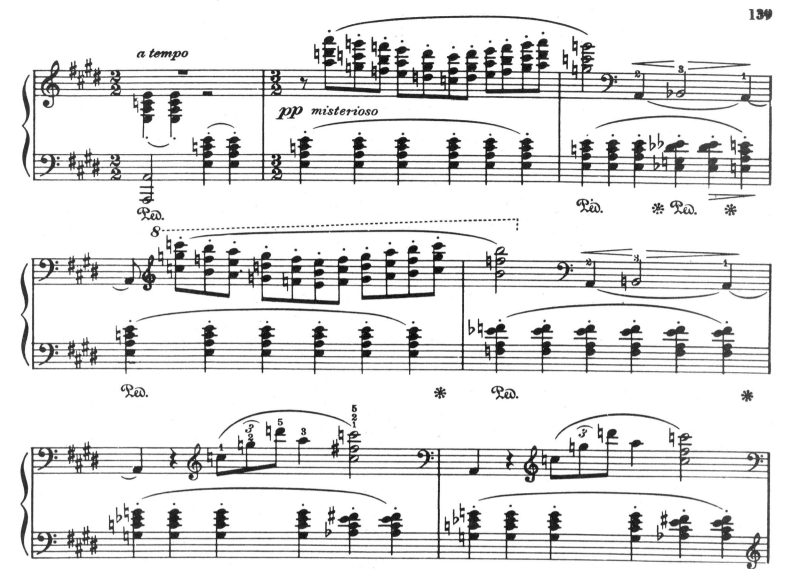

O3198

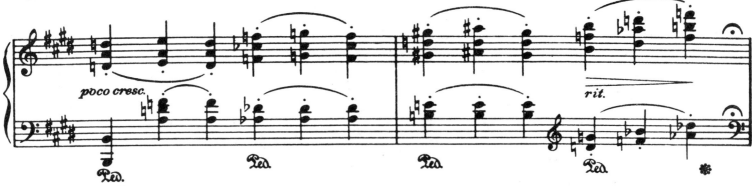

Lento e sostenuto

Tempo I

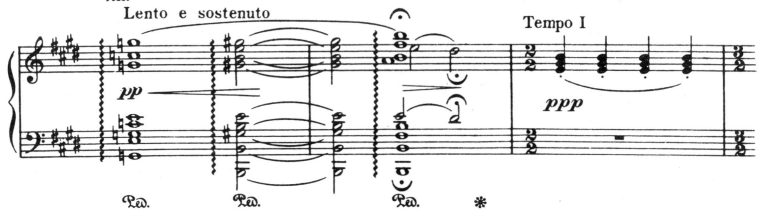

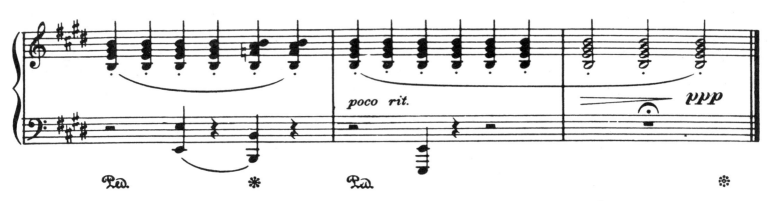

Polichinelle

SERGEI RACHMANINOFF, Op. 3, No. 4
(1873-1943)

Allegro vivace

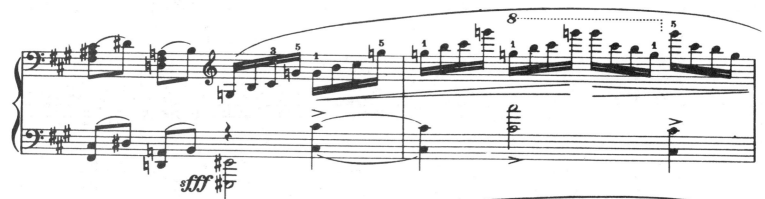

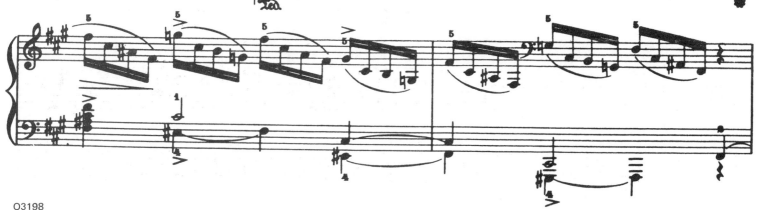

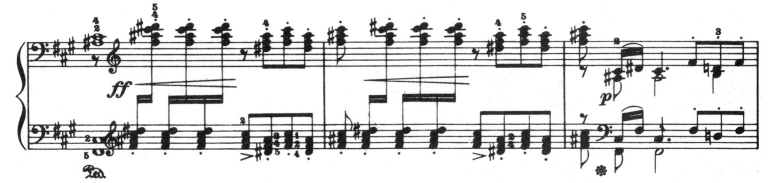

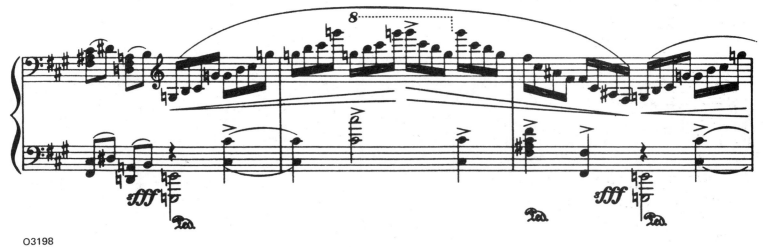

O3198

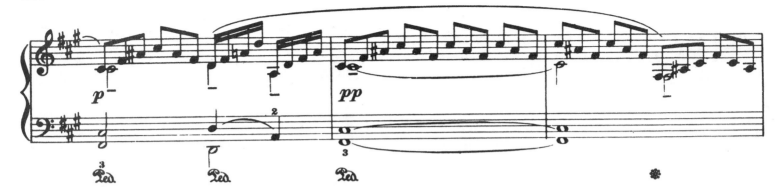

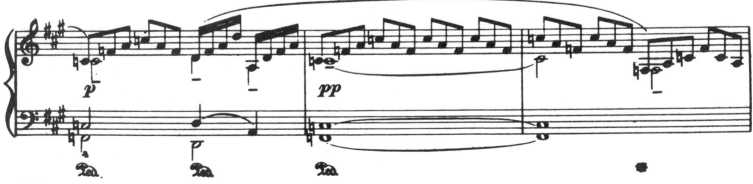

O3198

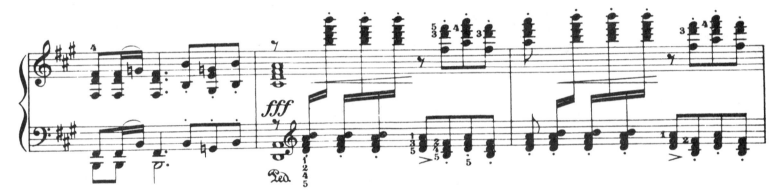

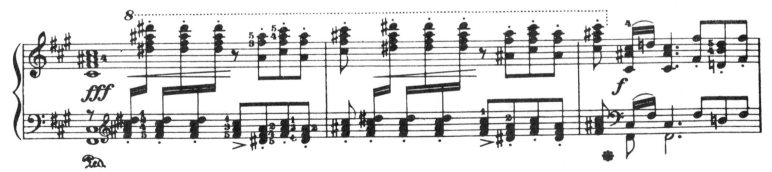

O3198

Romance

JEAN SIBELIUS, Op. 24, No. 9
(1865-1957)

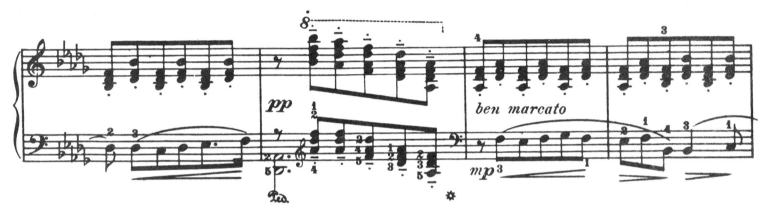

O3198

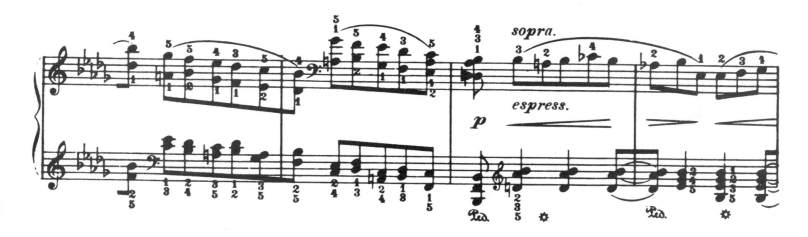

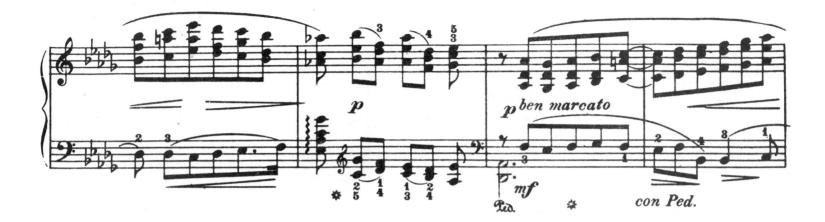

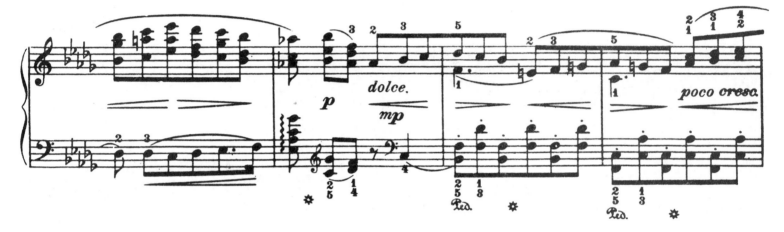

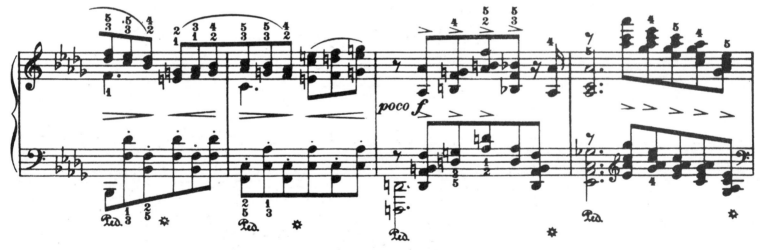

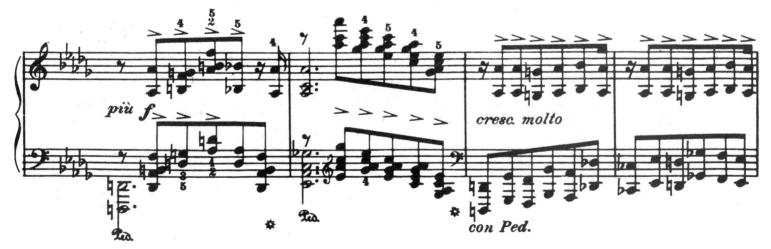

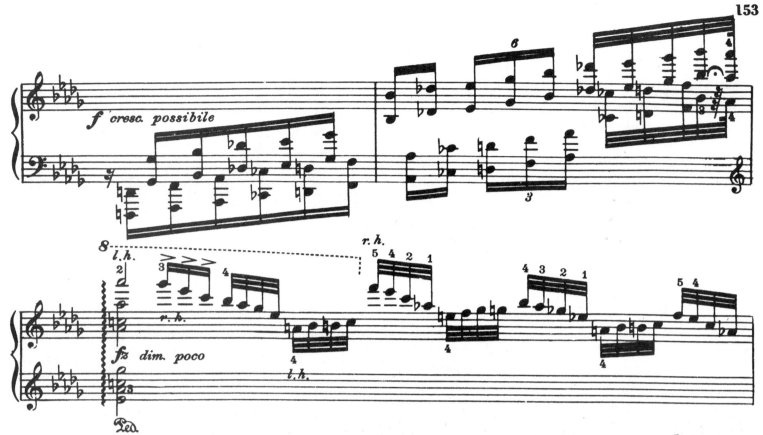

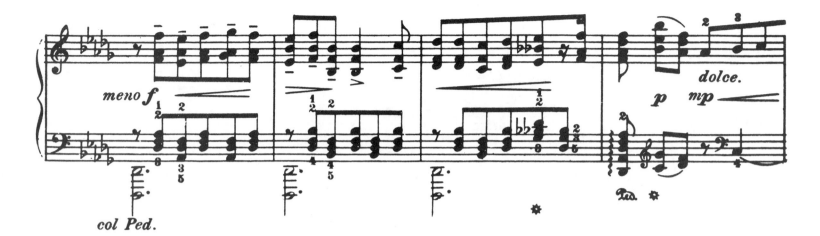

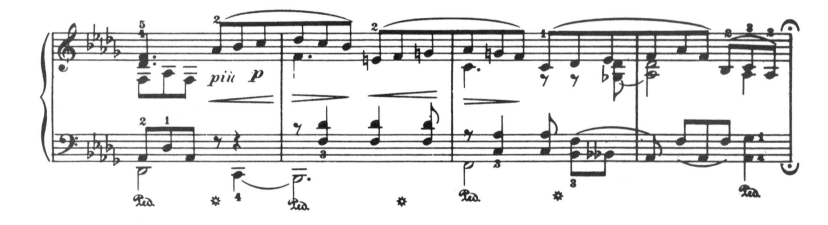

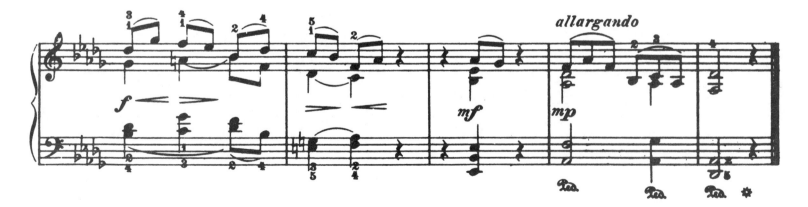

Rêverie

CLAUDE DEBUSSY
(1862-1918)

Andantino non lento

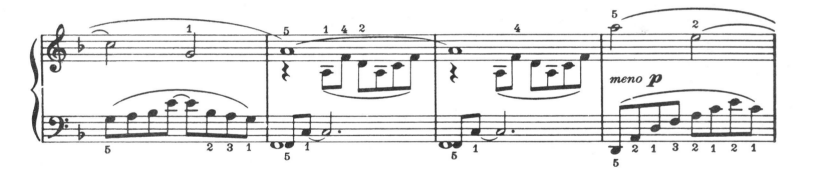

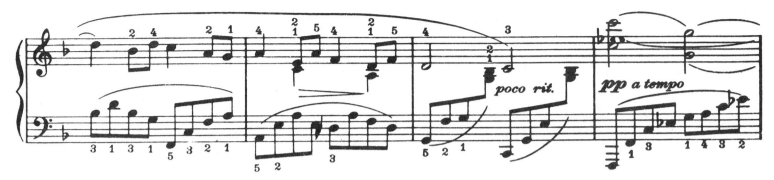

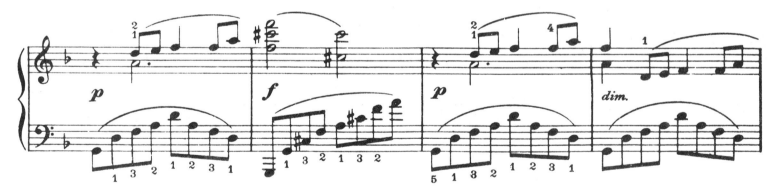

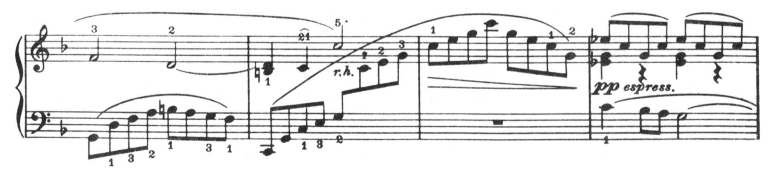

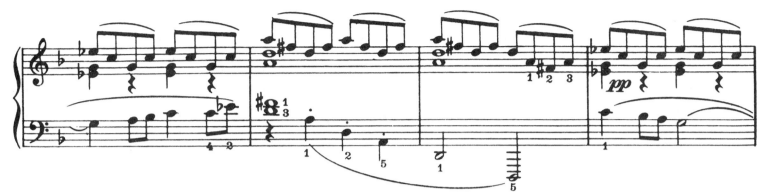

O3198

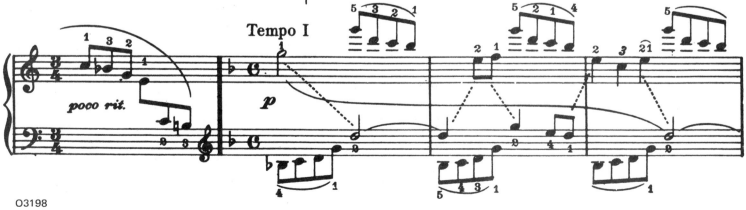

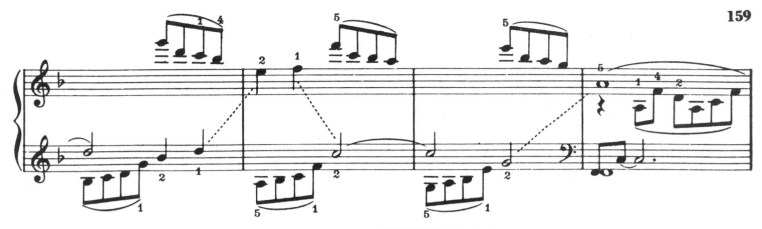

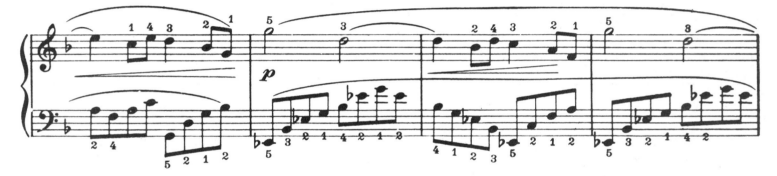

ALPHABETICAL INDEX OF TITLES

Page

Adagio from *Sonata* in C sharp Minor, "Moonlight" . . . . *L. van Beethoven* 12
Allegro from *Sonata* in C Major (K. 545) . . . . *W. A. Mozart* 16
Butterfly, The . . . . *E. Grieg, Op. 43, No. 1* 114
Czardas . . . . *V. Monti* 50
Dreams of Love (*Liebesträume*) . . . . *F. Liszt* 72
Fantasia (D Minor) . . . . *W. A. Mozart* 22
Flight of the Bumblebee . . . . *N. Rimsky-Korsakoff* 122
Hopak . . . . *M. Moussorgsky* 62
June (Barcarolle) . . . . *P. I. Tchaikovsky, Op. 37, No. 6* 106
May-Night . . . . *S. Palmgren, Op. 27, No. 4* 138
Menuet . . . . *I. J. Paderewski, Op. 14* 133
Minute Waltz . . . . *F. Chopin, Op. 64, No. 1* 36
Nocturne (E flat Major) . . . . *F. Chopin, Op. 9, No. 2* 90
Pastorale from *Sonata* No. 1 . . . . *D. Scarlatti* 8
Peter and the Wolf (Triumphal March) . . . . *S. Prokofieff, Op. 67* 78
Playera . . . . *E. Granados, Op. 5, No. 5* 94
Polichinelle . . . . *S. Rachmaninoff, Op. 3, No. 4* 141
Polonaise Militaire . . . . *F. Chopin, Op. 40, No. 1* 85
Praeludium . . . . *F. Mendelssohn* 117
Prelude and Fugue, First from *The Well-tempered Clavier*, Book I . . . . *J. S. Bach* 46
Prelude (C Minor) . . . . *F. Chopin, Op. 28, No. 20* 3
Prelude (C sharp Minor) . . . . *S. Rachmaninoff, Op. 3, No. 2* 127
Rêverie . . . . *C. Debussy* 155
Romance (E flat Major) . . . . *A. Rubinstein, Op. 44, No. 1* 111
Romance . . . . *J. Sibelius, Op. 24, No. 9* 150
Rondo alla Turca from Sonata in A Major (K. 331) . . . . *W. A. Mozart* 4
Rustle of Spring . . . . *C. Sinding, Op. 32, No. 3* 98
Scherzo (E Minor) . . . . *F. Mendelssohn, Op. 16, No. 2* 56
Spinning Song from *Song without Words* . . . . *F. Mendelssohn, Op. 67, No. 4* 28
Tango . . . . *I. Albeniz, Op. 165, No. 2* 33
Träumerei from *Scenes from Childhood* . . . . . . *R. Schumann, Op. 15, No. 7* 20
Valse triste . . . . *J. Sibelius, Op. 44* 66
Waltz in C sharp Minor . . . . *F. Chopin, Op. 64, No. 2* 40